ISBN: 0692531874
ISBN-13: 9780692531877

Published by: Communications Plus

Effervescent

Karen Bram Casady

"The more charming person is the person who admits the other person is more charming."
Benedict Cumberbatch

CONTENTS

My Dear Reader:

Muses come in many forms. According to dictionary.com, for the Romans, they were the nine daughters of Zeus and Mnemosyne who presided over various arts: Calliope (epic poetry), Clio (history), Erato (lyric poetry), Euterpe (music), Melpomene (tragedy), Polyhymnia (religious music), Terpsichore (dance) Thalia (comedy) and Urania (astronomy). For the purposes of this poetry, the muse will be defined simply as the inspiration behind the words that form the poetic tales expressed in this book. As the speaker in "Hound" says, "I shan't wave / I shan't knock." And so it will be for you my dear reader that the actual muse who very inadvertently and unknowingly provided the fodder from which these verses grew shall remain unnamed and hidden. Perhaps 'tis better that way. In so doing, it allows you an unfettered opportunity for further musing and surmising as you read the words; applying the poetic ideas as you see fit to your own reality. If you knew my muse, that possibility might never come to pass; you might be hindered in your interpretation. I shan't do that to you, my dear reader. KBC

Monarchy

My dear sir
What a solemn day it 'twas
Each word you uttered
Floated above the open tomb
Dangled momentarily
Executed a royal curtsy
As fitting a dead king's bones
Old and twisted
Rotten and rusted
Now lying in repose
Half a millennium old
Deposed and defeated
Tossed unmarked at Grayfriars
Duly suitable for a villainous usurper
Alleged murderer of young boys
In death slung over the back of a horse
Paraded naked through medieval streets
Alas perchance by the very creature for whom the bard would later have him beg
A horse, a horse!
My kingdom for a horse!
But your sonorous voice
Refined and melodious
Gave lift to the man
Syllable upon syllable descended
Benevolent sprites alighting
Each finding a delicate rib to cleanse
Ancient familial sinew bound you to him
Your eyes perhaps his eyes
His genome camouflaged in a strand of your hair
Concealing your tenuous royal roots
History's fragility held in your hands
Its continuum halted for a moment
You reach back through the ages and perfidies
Touch for an instant an ancient life
Pull it into wholeness
Return to it its dignity
Your soul rests against his
Forever bound up
You fall silent
Your given words spent

4

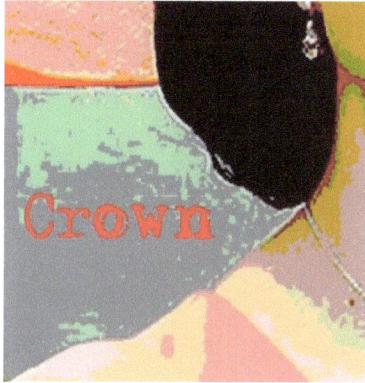

Crown

My dear madam
You took notice
Perhaps also moved by faded majesty
The thought of great bones arising
Seeking solace after half a millennium
Enduring battles modern and bygone
Satiating a hunger long put aside
Buoyed by decorous solemnity
A falsely rendered despot sanctuously laid to rest
Grand gestures meant to assuage distant Plantagenets
I reach back through centuries
Entreat a king
Ask a favor
A tract of land
Perchance a title as suited a cousin
Wondering when I am long dead
Will my skull be as his
Long in the cheekbones
Droll eye sockets
By the look knowing we were of the same blood
My voice cries out
His Highness hears nothing
But his soul echoes through me
Reverberates only once
Ringing my heart
Encircling it with gold
Leaving a crown
I bow
Hand over my chest
Grasp it and toss it upon you

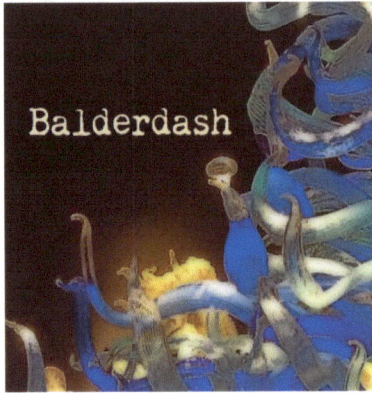

Balderdash

My dear sir
You interrupt my thoughts
Intrude upon my mindfulness
Fill my head with balderdash
You display extraordinary nerve
Prancing about
Festooning my brain with your handsomeness
Sprinkling it with your erudite hodgepodge
Distracting me
Leaving me dazed beyond succor
You sir create a bawdy hullabaloo
With your delicious carousing
And your luscious gallivanting
You leave me no peace
You traipse willy-nilly through my essence
Popping up in your spiffy raffish duds
Really sir I pray you
You torture me to the point of ribald cantankerousness and shameless debauchery
Your shenanigans rumble about my psyche upending all that is decent
Reducing me to a whirling tirade of insignificance
Then sir you amble off
Leaving one simple periwinkle
A small blue reminder to temper my foolishness
You lollygag as you go
Grinning and winking
Twirling about
And while I skedaddle to return to a semblance of propriety
Attempting to beget order out of your leftover ruckus
You tiptoe back and knock it all over again

Periwinkle

My dear madam
Ah yes
A simple periwinkle
Meant to soothe
To quiet your fuss
Giving you pause
An opportunity to measure
The depth of its blue
To count its petals
Their scent uncomplicated
And as you admire its delicate allure
From your pinnacle of madness
Amidst the balderdash
And the hodgepodge
My hands
Upon your fine bones
Alight a royal shimmer
Pouring across your entirety
Surging through capillaries
Warming the tips of fingers
The ends of toes
And in that moment
As your soul flames sapphire
You fall dazed
Beyond the succor of flowers
Upending all that is decent
Melting into my arms
Covering me with stunning cerulean ash

Hollywood Kiss

My dear sir
You simply must work on your Hollywood kiss
Your lips touch hers but
You hold back
Passion must pass between you
You mustn't contain it or
Guard it
Keeping it to yourself
Saving it
For someone else
Real or imagined
Perhaps afraid of its power
That once released
You may never take back
Forever lost to you
You must pretend that
She is yours
To take
To possess
All of her
She restlessly awaits
Release your fervor upon her
Complete her
Answer her
Convince us
The role requires it

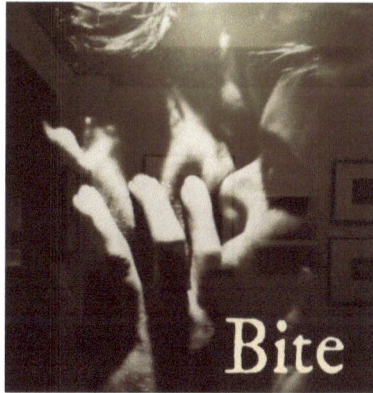

Bite

My dear madam
How dare you intrude upon my reputation
You presume to know how well I kiss based simply upon observation
You accuse me of holding back
Of moral restraint
Well madam j'accuse
For I am known to be a good kisser
I shall not simply press my mouth upon yours
Providing the politest of pecks
Or even a lengthy stray smooch
Instead I shall bite your lips
First a tender nibble
Our mouths slightly ajar
Absorbing the scent of your dinner
Tasting hints of chocolate and wine
Fueling my ardour and madness
Your lips bleed from passionate mayhem as I plunder them
My tongue slithers past reaching for your throat
You shan't breathe except for gasps
Then I shall retreat leaving you paralyzed with desire
Is this a true test
Perhaps not
Because you are not an actor
And this is not a mummer's play
I can do no less
Suffer the scene as it may
I shall render no Hollywood kisses upon your person
But shall save them for the imaginary world of thespians

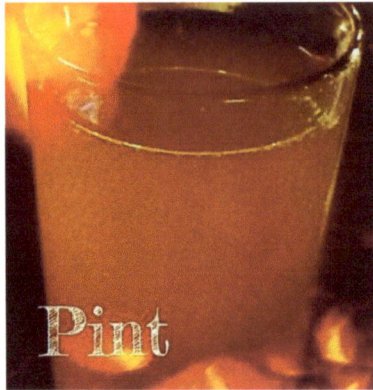

My dear sir
It seems I am coming to visit
Traveling a great distance
Seeking your company
And you shall say to me
Quite splendid
Most magnificent
A delicious surprise
I shall make time for you
Sort out a space
Fit you in
My current plans shall vanish, you shall say to me
The halls of my time shall become yours
Furnished with pleasures
Adorned with amusements
We shall dine on fine foods
Converse over succulent wines
Traipse about
Until our bones creak, you shall say to me
But sir, upon my arrival I shan't seek you out
I am not rude
I carry impeccable credentials of politeness
My chest heaves under the weight of etiquette
And sir, notification of my presence falls to you
I shall abide you nursing a fine pint at your accustomed public house
Earnest in the certainty of your destined appearance

Ebullient

My dear madam
You travel so far
Yet you shan't seek me out
This act or lack thereof puzzles me
For I have expected your visit for quite some time
Madam please do not stand on ceremony
Politeness burdens you
Weighs you down
Clouds your nimble wit
You stumble under the guise of etiquette
I shall abide by your wishes and seek you out
I desire your company, your banter and your dusky voice
You pretend that I do not
Imagining that I harbor indifference
That dispassion and aloofness govern me
When I come upon you
I shall offer my hand
Raise you into my embrace
Listen to your silly vain mockery
Laugh at the transparent badgering
Pouring from your rouged pursed lips
Silence them with a simple kiss
Ergo I shall take your arm in mine
Squire you about
Shoulder to shoulder
As we trip over our gaiety
Ebullient in our yearning
Finally falling through the threshold of my open door

Dung Beetle

My dear sir
Please tell me why you need a therapist
Perhaps too much
Too soon
The nuclear perks
Splendid
Sumptuous
Plentiful
Unforeseen and lovely
But alongside them
Inconvenient annoyances
Unwanted attention
Microscopic examination
Brooding over the impossible desire to accommodate
The difficult decisions ahead
Stay or go
Fly to greater heights
Soar to extraordinary
Shedding veracity
Or remain unexpected
By means of unpredictable honesty
And idiosyncratic quirkiness
Hovering just above unusual
Well sir
God speed
May your journey be mindful
And your process abundant
Dotted with awkward rewards and startling revelations
You must dig like a dung beetle
Past your quivering exoskeleton
Laying fertile eggs in palpable tissue
Finally encircling truth

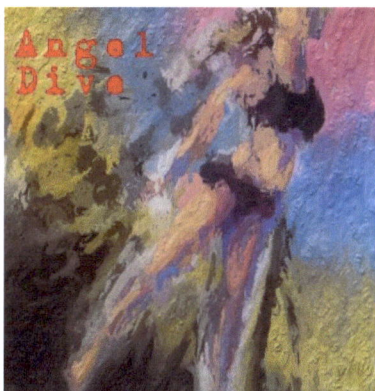

My dear madam
Your nosiness intrigues me
You ask me to trust you
Allow you past my hard-won persona
My dung beetle exoskeleton
That I permit you to angel dive into a crystal pool dyed red with clotted information
Choking you as you rise to its surface
Guided by false sunbeams peering through the muck
Pulling yourself through tendrils of random words and phrases
Meaningless to you
Slowing your rise
Clogging your throat and burning your lungs as you gasp for air
Suffocating you even as you reach out
And I must plunge in after you
For I know the way through my thoughts
Jumbled and dangerous
Like a giant hippo's crushing jaws
No place for a woman I tell you
But you plugged your ears with love
Now I must save you from drowning within me
And you struggle so
Pound my chest with your meager fists
Kick my shins through the thick drivel
Taking us to the murky bottom
Even as I retrieve our souls
But in the end
As you lie silky in my arms
Catching your breath
You unplug your love stuffed ears
And hear the beating of our hearts

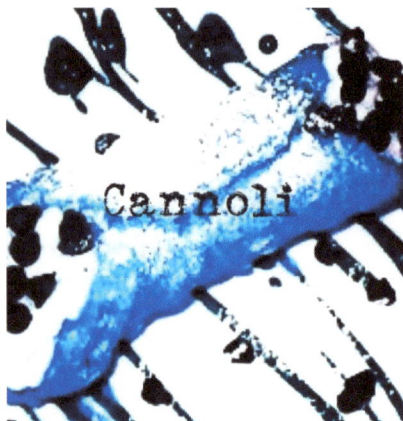

Cannoli

Dear
Sir
Did you
Really just
Taste for the first time
A fine Italian cannolo
Your trip to the city of Boston, Massachusetts
Has broadened your culinary outlook way past pub bangers and mash and shepherd's pie
Opened you up to the vast cuisine of agreeable sweet foods and your tongue to the sugary flavors of chocolate and vanilla crème
But dear sir I hope concern for your waistline denied you prior cannoli opportunities and not a lack of expansive gastronomic discernment or having an after dinner fling might be quite boring and dull

Fork

Dear madam
Cannoli
Such a silly name
For such a delicious treat
My first time
Yes
But it has come to my attention
That you too have never tasted a cannolo
Oh you've looked upon them with admiration
But the lusciousness of sweet ricotta and bits of chocolate
Wrapped in a round flakey shell has not yet passed your lips
Well madam
'Tis time for you to embark on your own culinary journey
Lest you lose sight of the prize
The wonderment your mouth shall endure
Your tongue wends its way through the smooth but mundane cream
It trips over a crumb
You play with it for a moment
Wondering
You bite
A tad of chocolate implodes
I watch your face
I lean close
I smell the deliciousness on your breath
See pleasure float through your eyes
How I must restrain myself
You take a second piece
Offer it up to my waiting mouth
The fork slides from my lips
I join your exaltation
Your gallivant through a heretofore unknown Sicilian paradise
A rhapsodic bliss of texture and sweetness
Its origins hinting at fertility
A celebration of ancient fecundity
Alas this desirous little tube
This cannolo leaves me spent

Persona

My dear sir
It appears you are an
Introvert trained as an extrovert
For your purposes
That works well
However
When you are not on stage
Hiding in your digs does not serve you
People talk
They wonder
You circumvent your fellow humans
Oh you may make brief forays out into the world
Sharing food
Sharing music
Sharing your body
But never sharing yourself
That remains a secret
Or so you think
Because people begin to surmise
Guess at your persona
Make assumptions
Sense a discomfort
Perhaps neediness
They begin to separate from you
Forget you
Put you into a little box from which there is no escape
And that sir
Does not serve you well at all

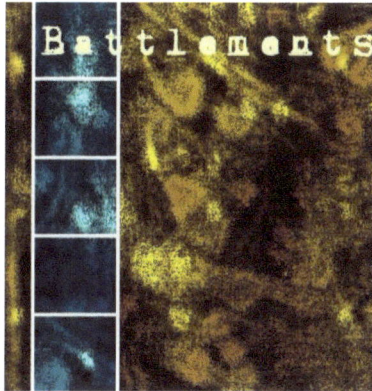

Battlements

My dear madam
Please join me in my box
The quiet deafens me
It grows to great proportions
May I offer you a plump slice of silence
Diced to luscious tidbits
To slide under your pink tongue
There to dissolve into silky midnight stillness
Seeping into me
Knowing my persona
Leaving no assumptions
Pedestrian as it seems
When I act you shall act
When I sleep you shall sleep
When I make love so shall you
And of the people who talk
Well my dear madam
Let their words bounce
From our smoldering battlements
Rebounding upon the wicked gossips
Drenching them with burning pitch
Filling their mouths and silencing them forever

Fairy Dust

My dear sir
It appears you have taken up residence in my neighborhood
On the very street where my hound and I walk daily
You picked a quiet virginal lane
Secluded but for the occasional car and a few pedestrians
The denizens who discovered this hidden urban gem
Who tiptoe through its celestial silence
Lest any noise attract unwanted attention
And you sir dodge the world in this perfect utopian refuge
Your splendid hideaway at the side of my sylvan path
Each morning I pass the faux French farmhouse where you bide your time
Working on whatever clever project occupies you
I linger for a singular moment
While the hound sniffs out her compatriots
I glance to the upper window and glimpse you at your endeavor
Certainly you see me for I sense recognition
Yet despite the possible outlet from your burdens
The opportunity to leave your concerns
You do nothing but remain deep in your mind
You fain familiarity as anathema to your being
I shan't wave
I shan't knock
Instead I speak to the nymphs and sprites who reside in the quiet lushness
Pleading for a tiny furor
An enchanted fairy dust storm
Of golden lust
And rising silver passion
But instead the hound finds a morsel
Pulls on the lead
And we walk on

Hound

My dear madam
I often look up from my work and out the window
And through the early morning haze of golden fairy dust
See you glide by my hideaway from whence I view the quiet green road below
My sylvan refuge shields me from all wandering eyes but yours
The big hound catches my attention
as she prowls along the lane
A tall blond with long legs
Somewhat resemblant of her companion
Elegant and free
Bold in her nuzzling
Shy with her glances
I see you look toward my window
But your focus is the hound
A magical rapport as you move in unison
Matched in repartee
Spellbound as if intoxicated by elfin elixirs
And you walk on
But I note a tiny glimpse over your shoulder at me
I nod but you've no notion of my small acknowledgement
Lost perhaps in a slight reflection of greenery against the pane

Retraction

My dear sir
I am a shameless wench
Intruding upon you
Desirous of your person
Wishing to know each detail of your life
Do you brush your teeth twice daily
Do your socks always match
What do you eat for breakfast
How do you take your tea
Selfish of me really
I cede you no mercy
I grant no quarter
But you pay no heed
And rightly so
You go forth
Pursue your life
Oblivious to me
Yet if given the chance
I'd bestow upon you my riches
The best of show
My spoils and plunder
Would that I knew sorcery
Could cast a spell
Infuse a potion
But 'tis fantasy
The stuff of magick
So I relent
Leave you to yours
Move on to mine

Misshapen

My dear madam
You wear a crooked crown
Don a tilted halo
Whichever you choose
Neither suffices
Both sit misaligned
Askew upon your head
You correct the lopsidedness
Twisting and adjusting
Manipulating each circlet
The mechanics defy you
Upon examination
No shortcomings sally forth
You inspect your skull
Feeling round and round
Probing with tender finger tips
Moving aside cowlicks and curls
You find nothing
One thing remains
Herein lies the solution
Your mind is misshapen
Buckled by overthinking
Bulging with indecision
Warped by ambiguity
Exploding with vagaries
Yet I wait to cull the unpleasantness
Guide you by my hand
Soothe your jaded mind
Set it straight with my heart
Even it out
Once again
Laying upon it your golden coronet and brilliant aura

Noise

My dear sir
Rest now
Lay ye down
Take a breath and survey your world
A bae soon arrives
Sending you topsy turvy
Scurrying after paraphernalia
The likes of which defy logic
That play with your tired brain
Spinning it in circles
Hurling it up and down the remains of your childhood
Holding sway over your essence
While in your sleep a tiny hand greets your fingers as they lay on her swollen belly
And you dream of winged flight
Apollo casting a golden shimmer
Drizzling sunlight across the azure vault
You share your soul through waves viscous with new life
Lulling you as you drown amidst lost sources of creation
Deep within the well of God's girth
As you drift along the River Styx toward the silence of long sleep
Over you go
Falling into dark rest
Stretched in quiet repose
The halls of life fading into entrails of nothing
And you begin again
Now immortal through microscopic bits of genes and chromosomes
Distilling into cognizance
Mutating into muscle and bone
Deciding between penis or vagina
But jarred awake you wonder what marvel is this?
You survey her sleeping form
Misshapen by impending bae
Crying out with love and horror
You soothe her but long for detachment
As you remove your long fingers from her fullness
And drift away
Solo

Ascend

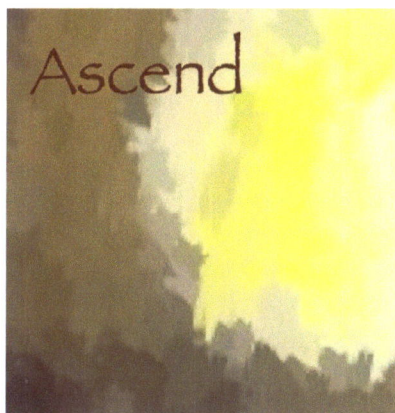

My dear madam
Rest indeed
Descend into quiet solitude
That I might dream of a golden bae
Touched by the Gods
Rendered invincible as Achilles
Blessed with the beauty of Helen
Elevated to Olympus
Far away from the River Styx
Where I often dwell
Communing with Dis'
Riding the Minotaur
Divining the song of the Harpies
I who have addressed dead kings
Played the roles of the thespian
I hold doubt above all
I ponder the prince or queen who floats in utero
The keeper of the future
Carrier of my immortality
For the beginning of this new life
Portends the end of mine
Bits of me shall go forth
Ride across the sky with the child
Ascend to its pinnacle
My wholeness turns away
Bound as it must
To fade into obsolescence and disuse
The day my bae is born is the day I see my own death I proclaim
No one but Charon the ferryman of Hades hears me

23

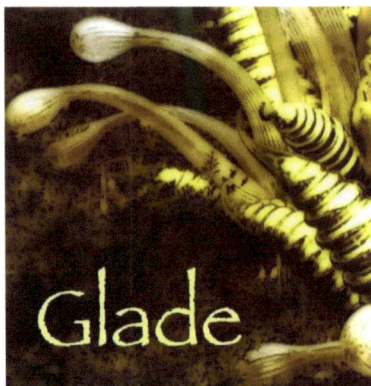

Glade

My dear sir
You take refuge in an ancient harbor town
Girded by mystic breakwaters
Whose timeworn antediluvian stones cry out with grayness and myth
You come alone
Piloting a small boat across sassy waves
Drawn by water nymphs and island sprites
Whispering breezes into your tired ears
Edging you away from visions of your new squalling bae
Promising you restful salvation and release
You fall asleep in a glade tickled by faerie ferns and pussy willows
Dreaming of life's continuum
Floating above it
Surveying its nooks and crannies
Taking it all in
You know the universe as God does
But you wake up in the hoary arms of a thicket
Bearing only the pinpoint knowledge of a mere speck
Imagining the faded cries of a woman in childbirth
The putrid mass between her legs
The demon chasing you from her side
Now only silence closes in
As you lie
In a glade
Beyond an ancient harbor town
Surrounded by mystic breakwaters
Whispering despair into your ears

Dis

My dear madam
You tell my story
You take me down a very dark path indeed
You illuminate my terror
Lay it bare
Cause me to reconcile
Come to terms and surrender
The light is where you are
Its glow purple and blue
Draw me to the hottest part of your flame
Pluck me from the thorny dark thicket
Relieve me of Dis' embrace
Use diamond shears to break my bonds
Golden cords to pull me free
Bind me up with purple silk
Surround my soul with your scent of lavender
Sweeten my fermented nostrils with vanilla
Allow me to return
To regain my vigor
And once again trod my path

Niche

My dear sir
I fear I put you in jeopardy
But 'twas no mistake
The story needed telling
Secrets fester and ooze
'Tis better to air them out
Set light upon them
Warm them
Deaden the rawness
Shrink the rent in your soul
Allow the truth a bearable place in your psyche
As a rolling marble finds its niche
Loosening grey matter as it settles
Shuddering then quieting
Stars scatter over parking lots
With your first steps home
Vow to remain immutable
Adhere to your truth
Waver not under great scrutiny
Now my dear sir
Slide your key into the door
And go henceforth

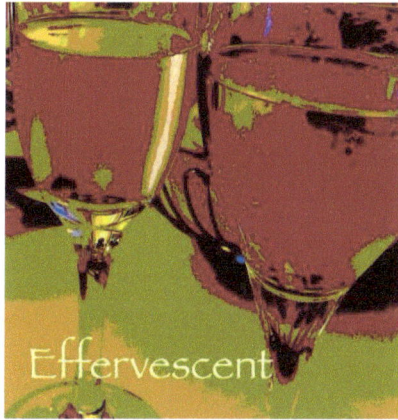

Effervescent

My dear madam
Your effervescent words pass between us
Splatter onto walls
Undulate from your mouth
Reverberate into my ears
Brilliant in their turns and combinations
Landing in my goblet
I swirl them
Sip them
Wash them down my throat with wine
Regurgitate utterances unbound into gibberish
Meaningless but for the whisper of your voice
Truth you do tell
Undispelled by even Bacchus
The key in my hand weighs heavy
Unlock the great door
Engraved with the past
Enter you say
'Twill be safe
I fell to the song of the Sirens
I fled the birth of my bae
Tempted by Mephistopheles
Dragged away by Harpies
But upon your word
I grasp my wretched heart
Return I must
My burden lies with my mistress
My truth with my progeny

About the Author

Karen Bram Casady, BA, MA is a journalist, business writer and editor, and a poet, short story writer and playwright. Over the course of her professional career she wrote and edited numerous publications, newsletters and magazines for large commercial clients. She edited and curated an award-winning collection of 100 stories, *Caring: Making a Difference One Story at a Time*. The book, created for Kaiser Permanente, sold more than 23,000 copies. Her poetry and short fiction appear in *Manuscript 46*, *Manuscript 47*, and *Manuscript 50*, the online literary journal of Los Angeles Valley College and *The Northridge Review*, the literary magazine of California State University, Northridge. Three of her five plays have been produced and she holds a membership in the Dramatists Guild. *Effervescent* represents her first published collection of poetry. Her other unpublished poetry collections include *Dailies*, *FridgeDoorPoetry*, *SlowDrive* and *SundryAsides*. She is a graduate of the University of Cincinnati (BA) and the University of Southern California (MA).

www.ingramcontent.com/pod-product-compliance
Lightning Source LLC
Chambersburg PA
CBHW041807040426
42448CB00005B/298